BRENT LIBRARIES

Please return/renew this item
by the last date shown.
Books may also be renewed by
phone or online.
Tel: 0115 929 3388
line www.brent.gov.uk/libraryservice

Ways into Science

Lifecycles

Peter Riley

FRANKLIN WATTS
LONDON•SYDNEY

Franklin Watts
Published in Great Britain in 2016
by The Watts Publishing Group

Copyright images © Franklin Watts 2015
Copyright text © Peter Riley 2015
(Text has previously appeared in *Ways into Science:
Lifecycles* (2003) but has been comprehensively
re-written for this edition.)

Editor: Julia Bird
Designer: Basement 68

ISBN: 978 1 4451 3483 3
Dewey classification number: 591.56

Printed in China

Franklin Watts
An imprint of
Hachette Children's Group
Part of The Watts Publishing Group
Carmelite House
50 Victoria Embankment
London EC4Y 0DZ

An Hachette UK Company
www.hachette.co.uk
www.franklinwatts.co.uk

Photo acknowledgements: All photos Roy Moller for Franklin
Watts except: Florian Andronache/Shutterstock: 13b.
BMJ/Shutterstock: 25b. Cheryl E. Davis/Shutterstock: 11b.
Torsten Dietrich/Shutterstock: 18b. Elenamiv/Shutterstock:
10r. Stephen Farhall/Shutterstock: 4, 12b. Gala_Kan/Shut-
terstock: 9br. Karel Gallas/Shutterstock: 5b, 25t. Toni Genes/
Shutterstock: 20t, 20b. Grey Carnation/Shutterstock: 22.
Daniel Heuclin/NHPA: 19b. Hornpipe/Dreamstime: front
cover c, 16b. Irin-k/Shutterstock: 10c. Eric Isselee/Shutterstock:
17c, 17b, 18t, 27tr. Heiko Kiera/Shutterstock: 3, 19t, 27cr.
King Tut/Shutterstock: 24t. Kosan/Shutterstock: 23c. Doug
Lemke/Shutterstock: 5t,15. Harmut Morgenthal/Shutterstock:
13t. Oksana 2010/Shutterstock: 11t. Picturepartners/
Shutterstock: 27bl. PRILL/Shutterstock: 5ca, 17t.
Pureradiancejennifer/Dreamstime: front cover b. Leena
Robinson/Shutterstock: 24b. Benjamin Sieneta/Shutterstock:
23tr, 27tl. Sofiaworld/Shutterstock: 27br. Vasily Vishnevskiy/
Shutterstock: 5c, 21t, 21b. Bob Watkins/Photofusion: 6l, 6r, 7t,
7bl, 7br. Barrie Watts: 14. Sarah Z/Shutterstock: 12t.
Roberto Zocchi/Shutterstock: 27bc.

Every attempt has been made to clear copyright.
Should there be any inadvertent omission,
please apply to the Publishers for rectification.

Contents

What is a lifecycle?

All living things have a lifecycle.
There are different stages in
a lifecycle.

Many living
things are born.

They grow.

They change.

They can
have young.

They grow old
and then they die.

Plants

The lifecycle of a plant starts when its seed sprouts.

Tom has put some pea seeds in soil.

He waters them.

Soon seedlings grow out of the seeds.

The seedlings grow taller and become plants with leaves.

Tom plants them outside.

Buds form on the plants.

?

What do you think the buds will grow into? Turn the page to find out.

Flowers and seeds

A flower grows out of each bud. Flowers make nectar for bees to feed on.

Flowers also make pollen. Bees carry it between the flowers as they feed on the nectar.

Plants use the pollen to make seeds.

10

The seeds scatter and grow into new plants.

Some plants then die. Others grow new flowers again next year.

Some trees can live for hundreds of years.

seeds

Insects

Ben has found some eggs on a leaf.

He looks at the eggs every day. One day, he finds tiny caterpillars have hatched from the eggs.

The caterpillars eat leaves and grow bigger.

When one of the caterpillars is fully grown, it sheds its skin. It turns into a pupa (sometimes called a chrysalis).

What do you think happens next? Turn the page to find out.

13

A butterfly

butterfly

Inside the pupa, more changes take place. The caterpillar is changing its form.

One day, the pupa splits open and a butterfly comes out.

The butterfly feeds on nectar in flowers.

It lays some eggs. Soon after, the butterfly dies.

What other creatures change a lot in their lifecycle? Turn the page to see one example.

Amphibians

Amphibians change a lot in their lifecycle.

Emily has some frog spawn from a pond. Frog spawn is made of eggs and jelly.

The eggs are black. The jelly is clear. You can see through it.

16

Emily looks at the frog spawn every day. One day, she sees tadpoles hatching from the eggs.

The tadpoles start to grow and change shape. They grow back legs.

Then they grow front legs.

What do you think happens next? Turn the page to find out.

Frogs

The tadpoles' tails shrink. They change into froglets.

The froglets leave the water and live on land.

In time, they become frogs. In a few years, they can make frog spawn too.

18

Reptiles

The lifecycle of a reptile starts with an egg.

When reptiles are fully grown, they lay eggs themselves.

What other creatures begin life inside an egg? Turn the page to find out.

Birds

Birds start
life as eggs.

Chicks hatch
out of the eggs.

The parents feed their chicks in the nest.

When the chicks are grown, they make nests and raise chicks themselves.

Mammals

Harry has a cat called Tibby. Tibby has kittens.

The kittens feed on their mother's milk. This helps them to grow.

Harry weighs each kitten every week. He records their weight.

He makes a chart of a kitten's growth. What do you think it will show?

The kittens will become adult cats after about ten months.

What animals do you find on a farm? Turn the page to find out.

500 0 500
9   1
10kg
8   2
7   3
6 5 4
500 500

Farm animals

You find chicks on a farm. Chicks hatch from eggs. What do they grow into?

What do you think this young bird will grow into?

Lambs are born in the spring. What do they grow into?

Calves are often born in the spring and summer. What do they grow into?

What other animals might you find on a farm? What are their young called?

What stage?

Look at the photos opposite. What stage in a lifecycle does each one show?

Make a table like this and fill it in.

Photo	Starting out	Growing up	Having young
Kitten	✗	✓	✗
Tadpole	?	?	?
Seedlings	?	?	?
Snake	?	?	?
Seeds	?	?	?
Butterfly	?	?	?
Swan	?	?	?

kitten

tadpole

snake
hatching

seedlings
growing

seeds

butterfly

Swan with nest

Useful words

Amphibians – animals such as frogs, toads and newts that start their lifecycle in water but change into different body shapes before moving out of the water to live on land. Amphibians always return to water to lay their eggs.

Bird – an animal covered in feathers with a pair of wings.

Buds – green lumps on stalks or twigs that can grow into flowers, leaves or stems.

Butterfly – an insect with two pairs of wings covered in scales which are often brightly coloured.

Egg – the first stage in the lifecycles of animals such as birds and frogs.

Flower – the part of a plant where seeds are made.

Milk – the liquid food that baby mammals drink directly from their mothers.

Nectar – a sweet liquid that plants make that bees, some other insects and some birds drink.

Pollen – a yellow powder that helps flowers to make seeds.

Reptiles – a group of animals with dry, scaly skin. Lizards, snakes, tortoises and crocodiles are reptiles.

Seed – the first stage in the lifecycle of a plant.

Seedlings – young plants that have just started to grow from seeds.

Some answers

Here are some answers to the questions we have asked in this book. Don't worry if you have some different answers to ours; you may be right too. Talk through your answers with other people and see if you can explain why they are right.

Pages 6–7 Discuss how people change over time.

Pages 20–21 Discuss how birds change over time and refer to local observations of birds using nest boxes and feeding chicks. Make sure that if children discover a bird's nest, they leave it alone so the parents can care for their eggs and young.

Page 23 The chart would show that the kitten's weight increases steadily until it is fully grown.

Pages 24–25 The chicks will grow into chickens. The young bird will grow into a duck. The lambs will grow into sheep. Calves will grow into cows and bulls. Other farm animals could include pigs and piglets, goats and kids, horses and foals, geese and goslings.

Page 26 These are the answers for the table. Starting out: Seeds and the snake that is hatching out. Growing up: seedling, kitten and tadpole. Having young: the butterfly and the swan. The butterfly is an adult insect and fully grown so the next stage for it is to have young. The swan has laid eggs and is having young.

Conservation note: All activities involving collection and care of living things must be in accordance with school policies.

Index

About this book

Ways into Science is designed to encourage children to think about their everyday world in a scientific way and to make investigations to test their ideas. There are five lines of enquiry that scientists make in investigations. These are grouping and classifying, observing over time, making a fair test, searching for patterns and researching using secondary sources.

• When children open this book they are already making one line of enquiry – researching about lifecycles. As they read through the book they are invited to make other lines of inquiry and to develop skills in scientific investigation.

• On pages 6–7 the children can observe how people change over time.

• On pages 8–9 the children use their observations and ideas to suggest answers and make a prediction.

• On pages 12–15 the children observe how an insect changes over time. They use their observations and ideas to suggest answers and make a prediction.

• On pages 16–18 the children observe how an amphibian changes over time. They use their observations and ideas to suggest answers and make a prediction.

• On pages 20–21 the children can observe how birds change over time.

• On page 23 the children see how the change in weight of a kitten is measured over time. They see how data is gathered and recorded and are asked to make a prediction.

• On page 26 they should make a copy of the table and use the pictures on page 27 to fill it in after making judgments on the stages in the lifecycles of the plants and animals shown.